McGraw-Hill Social Studies

Cleo H. Cherryholmes
Lynn Cherryholmes
Gary Manson
Peter H. Martorella
Rosemary Messick
Anna Ochoa
Joyce Speas
Jan L. Tucker
June Tyler
George Vuicich

PROGRAM CONSULTANTS

LAURENCE W. ARONSTEIN
Principal, Memorial School
Millis Elementary Schools

MADGE BARNETT
Former Social Studies Consultant
Richardson Schools, Texas

JOANNE BUGGEY
Social Studies Consultant
Minneapolis, Minnesota

GEORGE W. FRENCH
Director, Social Studies
Philadelphia Public Schools

RITA IRONS
Educational Consultant
Westport, Connecticut

MARK LYTLE
Department of History
Bard College

JOHN D. McAULAY
Emeritus of Education
Pennsylvania State University

ANTHONY PETRILLO
Director of Instruction
Jefferson County Schools

VINCENT PRESNO
Department of Curriculum and
Instruction
Wright State University

PETER R. SENN
Department of Economics and Social
Science
Wilbur Wright College

BARBARA VORNDRAN
Career Education Specialist
Teachers College, Columbia
University

BETTY J. WICKRE
Countryside Elementary School
Edina, Minnesota

CONTENT CONSULTANTS

FELIX D. ALMARAZ, JR.
Associate Professor of History
The University of Texas of
San Antonio

J.G. BRADLEY
Department of Education in the Social
Sciences
McGill University

JOANNE CHANCEY
Consultant on Early Childhood Education
Florida State Department of Education

KAREN L. MOHR CHAVEZ
Department of Sociology and
Anthropology
Central Michigan University

MARIO R. daCRUZ
Education Specialist
São Paulo, Brazil

JOSEPH DECAROLI
Department of Curriculum and
Instruction
Newark, Delaware

RAMIRO GARCIA
Bilingual Consultant
Los Angeles City Unified School District

JUDY GILLESPIE
Social Studies Development Center
Indiana University

JOHN T. GULLAHORN
Department of Sociology
Michigan State University

JOHN HOSTETLER
Department of Anthropology
Temple University

MARI-LUCI JARAMILLO
American Ambassador to Honduras
American Embassy, Tegucigalpa

JANET LOPE
Administrator
Bureau of Indian Affairs
Shiprock, New Mexico

JAN M. MATELY
Department of Geography
Michigan State University

C.W. MINKEL
Principal Representative of Michigan
State University at the
Brazilian Ministry of Education
Brazilia, D.F. Brazil

ALFRED E. OPUBOR
Center for African Studies
Michigan State University

LOUISE SAUSE
Department of Early Childhood
Michigan State University

ENID SCHILDKROUT
Department of Anthropology
The American Museum of Natural History

HARRIET SKYE
Office of Public Information
United Tribes Educational Technical
Center
Bismarck, North Dakota

EDOUARD TAPSOBA
Ministry of Planning and Rural
Development
Republic of Upper Volta, Africa

JACK F. WILLIAMS
Department of Geography
Michigan State University

CLASSROOM CONSULTANTS

JANE KANNE
Logan Elementary School
Los Angeles, California

ANN WILSON
Garfield School
Elgin, Illinois

NANCY PINNELL
New Pitman School
Kirkwood, Missouri

VIRGINIA FRIDDELL
Meadowbrook Elementary School
Norfolk, Virginia

MARY LINLEY
Western Avenue School
Geneva, Illinois

KENNETH SHERWOOD
Kings Highway Elementary School
Westport, Connecticut

ANN PITSTICK
Swift Elementary School
Arlington, Texas

Discovering Others

BY
Peter H. Martorella
*Professor,
Social Studies Education
Temple University*

Cleo Cherryholmes
*Department of Political Science
Michigan State University*

Gary Manson
*Department of Geography
Michigan State University*

WEBSTER DIVISION, McGRAW-HILL BOOK COMPANY

New York   St. Louis   San Francisco   Auckland   Bogotá   Düsseldorf
Johannesburg   London   Madrid   Mexico   Montreal   New Delhi
Panama   Paris   São Paulo   Singapore   Sydney   Tokyo   Toronto

Editorial Development:

Senior Editor: Paul Hastings Wilson
Project Director: Len Martelli
Editors: Marlena M. Baraf, Mary Ann Demers, Cathy Kellar
Editing and Styling: Sal Allocco, Diana Ober, Patricia L. McCormick
Design Supervision: Lisa Delgado, Bennie Arrington
Photo Research: Suzanne Volkman
Production Supervisor: Karen Romano
Consultant: Alma Graham, Founding Member, Textbook Committee, NOW-NY
Design: Graphic Arts International
Cover Photo: Beatrice Pinsley/Image Bank

Library of Congress Cataloging in Publication Data
Martorella, Peter H
  Discovering others.
  (McGraw-Hill social studies)
  Includes index.
  SUMMARY: A first-grade textbook examining families, social environment, and some of the cultural traditions of our country.
  1. Social perception—Juvenile literature.
2. United States—Social conditions—Juvenile literature. 3. National characteristics, American—
Juvenile literature. [1. Social perception.
2. United States—Social conditions] I. Cherryholmes, Cleo H. II. Manson, Gary. III. Title.
HM132.M347   973   78-1880
ISBN 0-07-011916-3

Acknowledgments are an extension of this copyright page and are found on page 128.

COPYRIGHT © 1979 BY McGRAW-HILL, INC. All Rights Reserved. Printed in the United States of America. No part of this publication may be reproduced, stored in a retrieval system, or transmitted, in any form or by any means, electronic, mechanical, photocopying, recording, or otherwise, without prior written permission of the publisher.

ISBN: 0-07-011916-3

CONTENTS

UNIT ONE — ME AND YOU

Looking At Me and You 10 ■ I Am Special 14 ■ All About Me 18 ■ What Do I Like? 20 ■ What Have I Done? 24 ■ I Wish 28 ■ How Do I Feel? 30 ■ What Makes Me Feel This Way? 32 ■ Leave Me Alone 34 ■ What Do I Think? 36 ■ What Would I Feel? 38 ■ What Should I Do? 40 ■ Alone or with Others 42 ■ We Need Each Other 44

UNIT TWO — ME AND OTHER PEOPLE

How Do I See People? 48 ■ How Do We Change? 50 ■ How Do We Tell Each Other Things? 54 ■ What Did You Say? 58 ■ What Would We Like to Be? 60 ■ You Hurt Me 64 ■ What Would I Do? 66 ■ A Promise 68 ■ What's Fair? 70 ■ What Will Happen? 72

UNIT THREE — MY FAMILY AND MY NEIGHBORHOOD

What Is a Family? 78 ■ What Do Family Members Need? 82 ■ What Do Family Members Do for One Another? 84 ■ What Do Families Do Together? 86 ■ Where Do Families Live? 88 ■ What Is All around Me? 92 ■ A School 94 ■ School Neighborhood 96 ■ A Community 98 ■ Community Workers 100

UNIT FOUR

MY COUNTRY

We Are Americans 104 ■ Our Capital 106 ■ Special Days 108 ■ What Do Americans Look Like? 110 ■ Who Are Native Americans? 112 ■ Americans Came from Many Lands 114 ■ Many Different Foods 116 ■ Getting to School 118 ■ School Then and Now 120 ■ Cooking Breakfast 122 ■ When I Grow up 124

UNIT ONE

Me and You

Looking at Me and You

Look at these children.
How are these children alike?

How are these children different?

Look at these people, too.
How are these people alike?

How are these people different?

I Am Special

I am Pat.
These pictures are about me.

These are some things I like to do.

I am Paul.
These pictures are about me.

These are some things I like to do.

All about Me

This is Angela.
This page tells about Angela.

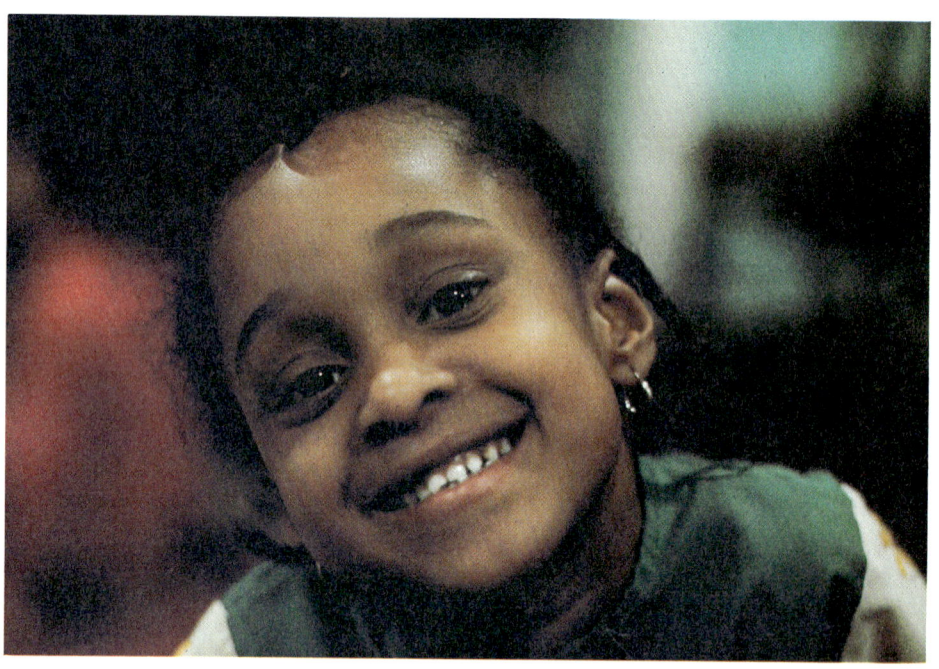

All About Me

My name is ANGELA LINDSEY.

I like to be called ANGEL.

My birthday is MAY 26, 1973.

I live at 12 HILLSIDE DRIVE.

I have 1 brothers and 0 sisters.

I go to W. H. REED School.

This is Angela's friend, David.
Angela wrote these things about David.

About Someone I Know

DAVID is my _FRIEND_.

DAVID likes to be called _DAVE_.

DAVID was born _ON JUNE 10, 1973_.

DAVID lives at _27 HILLSIDE DRIVE_.

DAVID has _1_ brothers and _1_ sisters.

DAVID goes to _W. H. REED_ School.

What Do I Like?

This is Maryanne.
Maryanne likes many things.

These are Maryanne's favorite things.

This is Henry.
Henry loves to eat.

These are some of his favorite things.

What Things Have I Done?

What are these children doing?

Have you done any of these things?

What are these children doing?
Have you done any of these things?

What would you like to do?

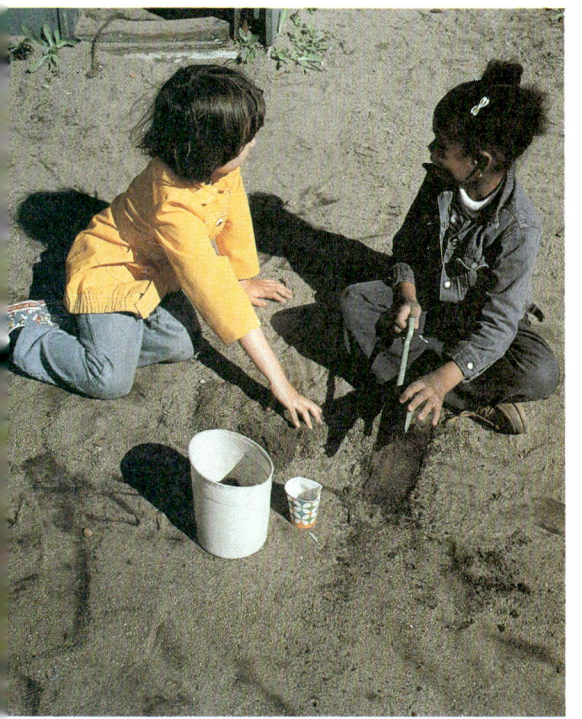

These children have found a genie.
The genie will give them one wish.

What are the children's wishes?

How Do I Feel?

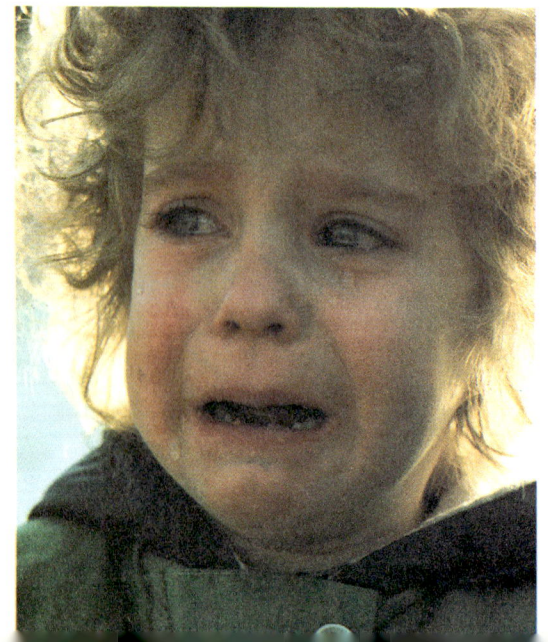

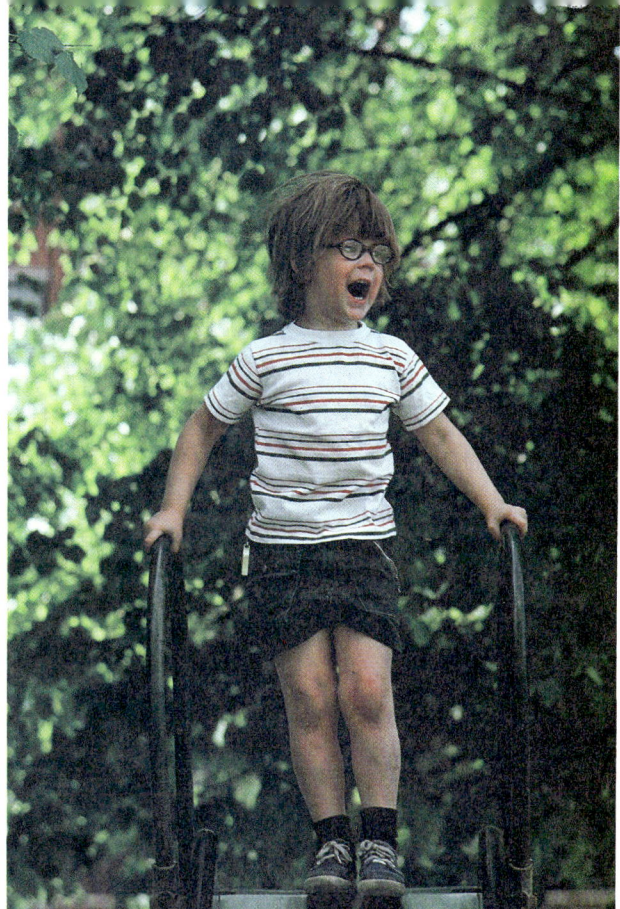

How do these people feel?
How can you tell?

What Makes Me Feel This Way?

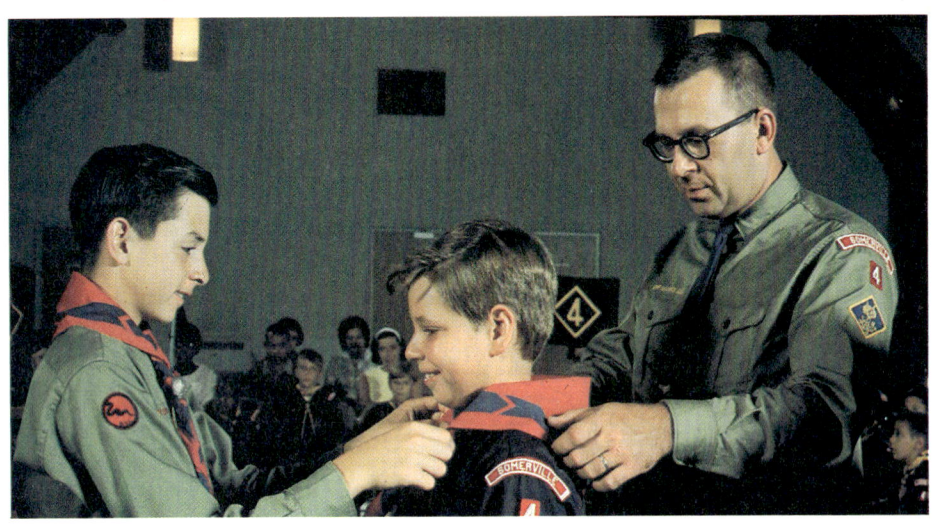

These children are proud.

Do these children look proud?
What are they doing?
How do they feel?

Leave Me Alone

34

These children feel shy.
How can you tell?
What makes them feel this way?

35

What Do I Think?

This boy is new in school.
How do you think the boy feels?

Kim is six years old.
Her sister just won a prize.
How does Kim feel?

What Would I Feel?

What is the boy doing?
Why is the girl laughing?

38

What is happening in this picture?
What is the boy feeling? Why?

What Should I Do?

What are these children doing?
Should their friends do the same things?

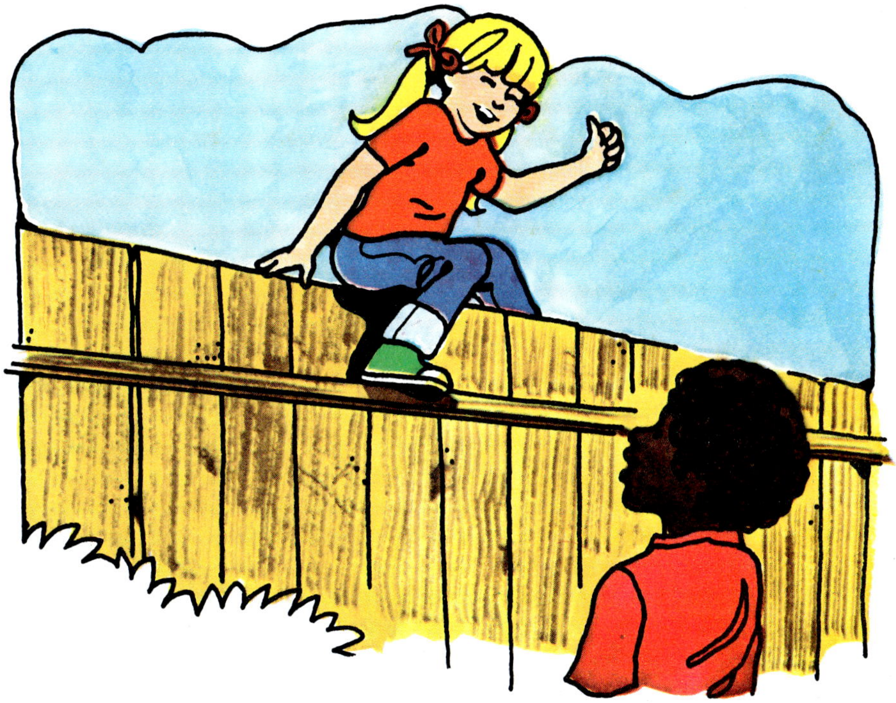

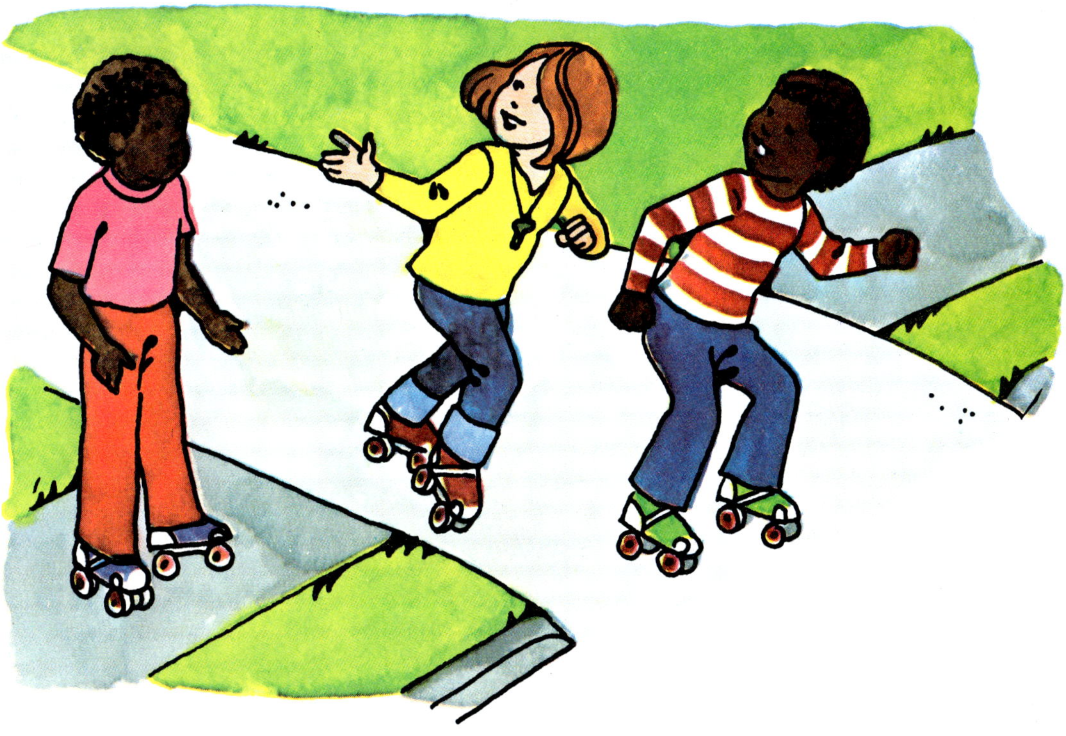

Alone Or With Others

What are these children doing?

Which children are doing things alone?
Which are doing things with others?

43

We Need Each Other

What are these people doing?

Why do these people need each other?
Could they do these things alone?

UNIT TWO

Me and Other People

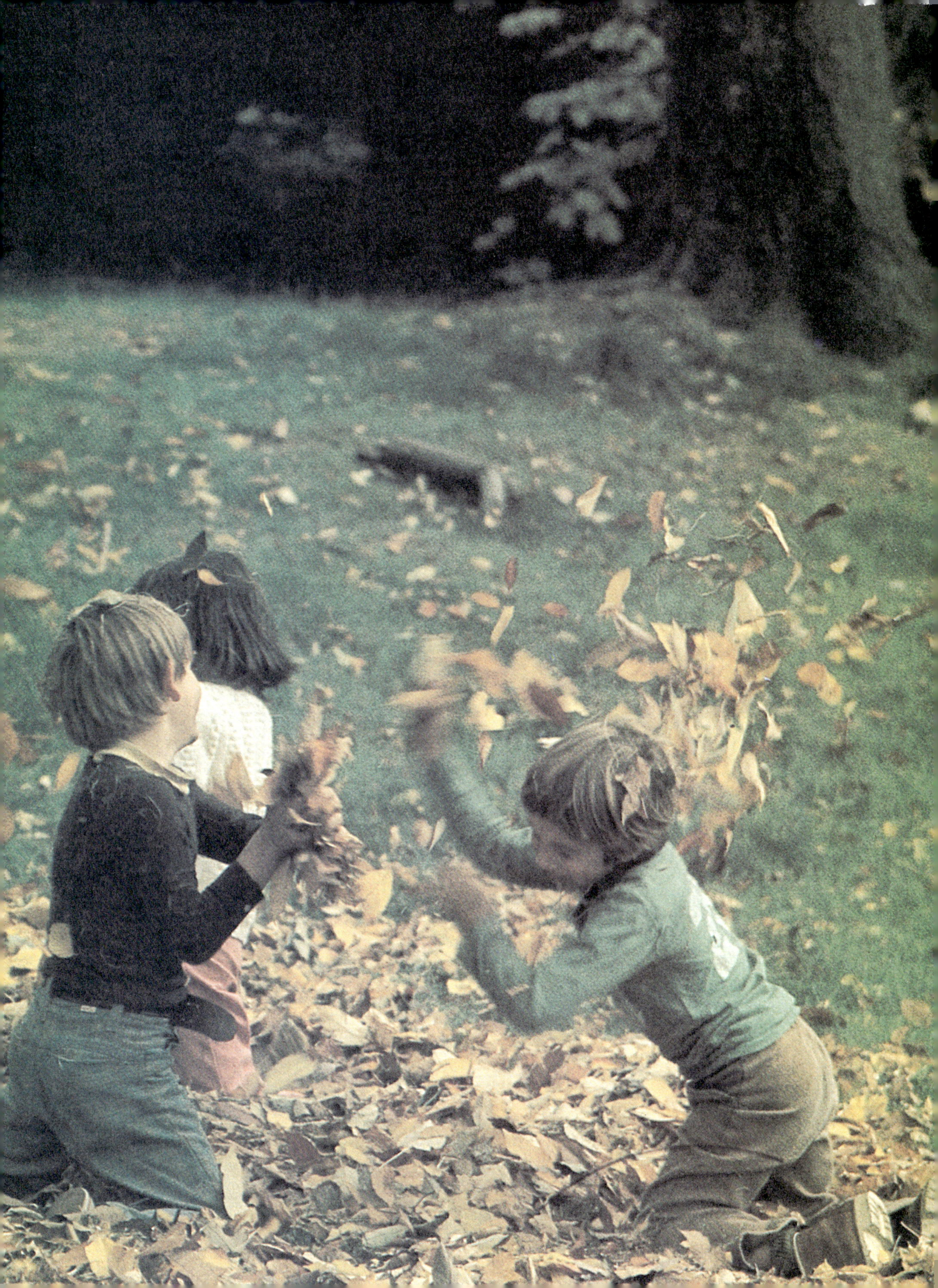

How Do I See People?

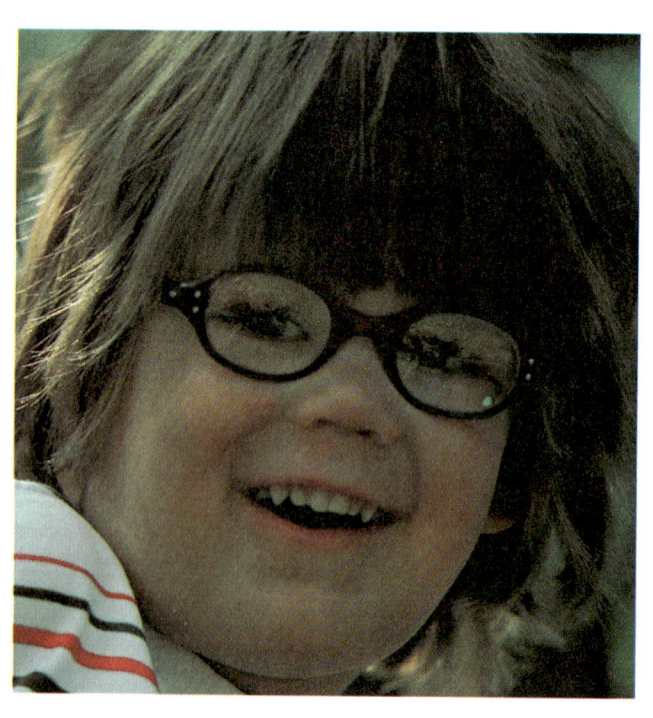

49

How Do We Change?

This is Ann.

She is a baby.

Now she crawls.

Now she walks.

This is Ann in the first grade.

This is Ann.
How old is Ann in each picture?

What is Ann doing?
What thing can Ann do now?

How Do We Tell Each Other Things?

Some of these people are sending messages.
Some of these people are getting messages.

54

How are they sending and getting messages?

What are these people telling us?
How are these people sending messages?
How are these people getting messages?

57

What Did You Say?

Are these children listening?
How can you tell?
Will anyone learn?

The children are listening.
How can you tell?
How do you listen?

What Would We Like To Be?

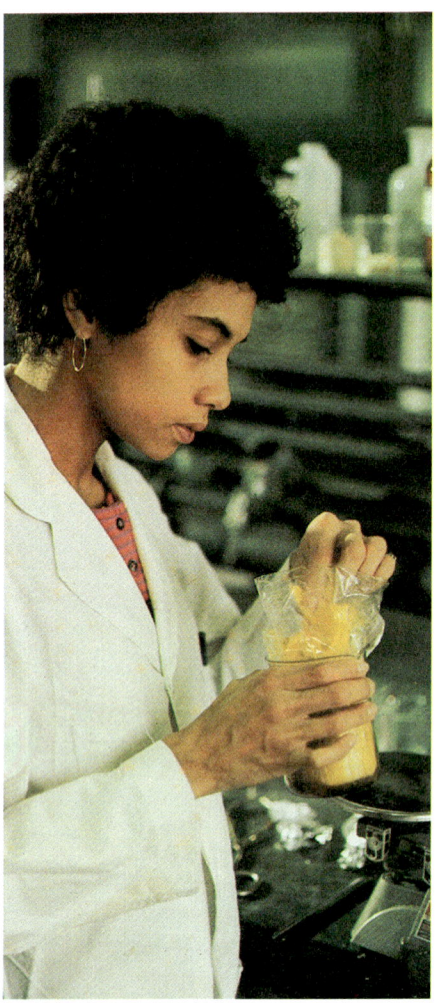

These people are working.
What kind of work do they do?

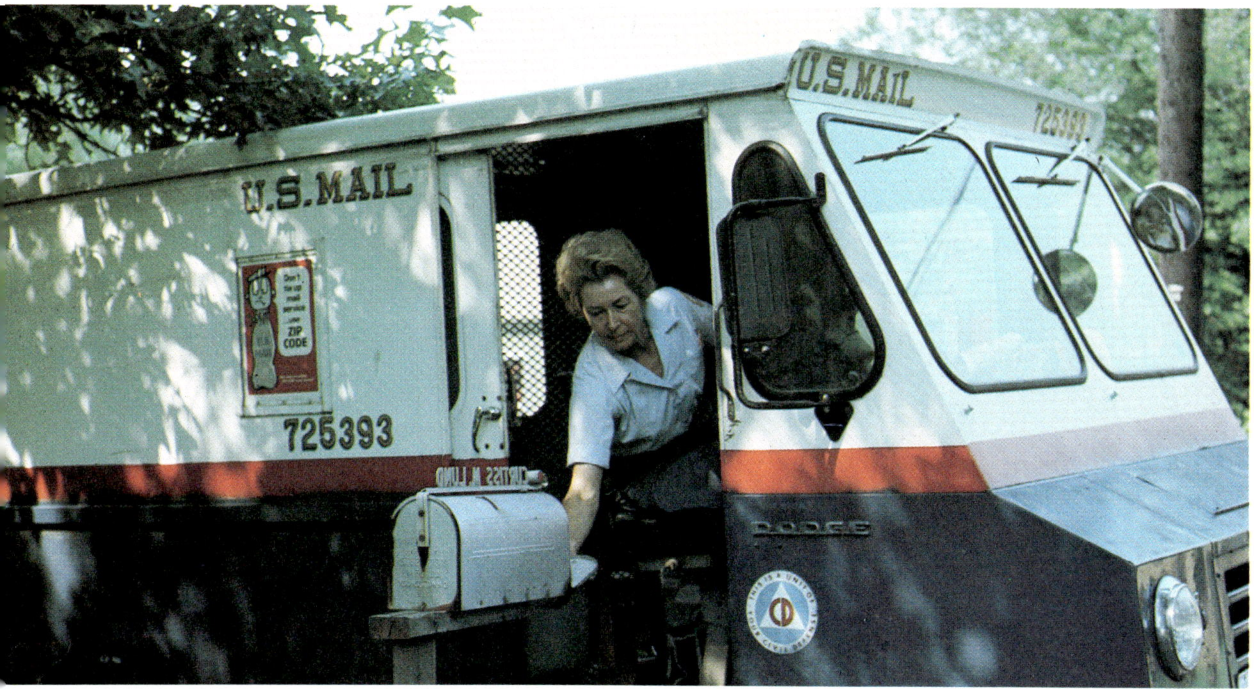
U.S.MAIL
725393
U.S.MAIL
725393
ZIP
CODE
DODGE

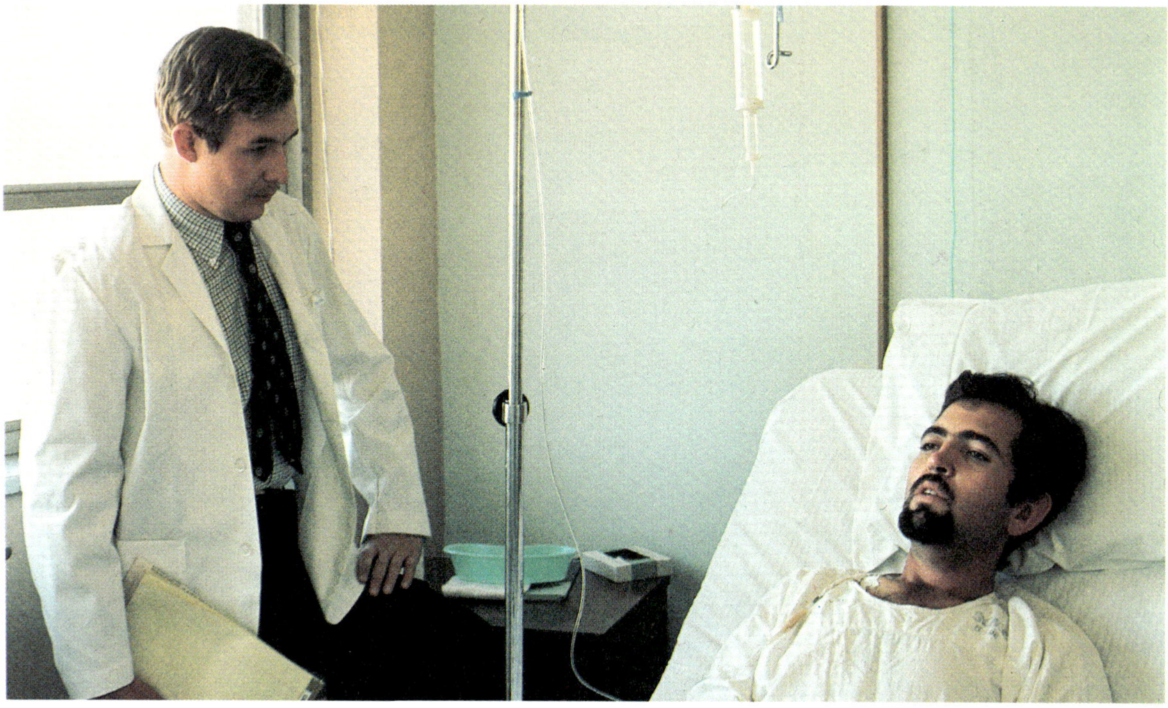

Here are more people working.
What kind of work do they do?

Would you like to do what they do?

You Hurt Me!

Roger is playing with some blocks.
Maria wants to play, too.
Roger says he wants to play alone.
Maria knocks down the blocks.

Roger pushes Maria.
What does Mother do?

65

What Would I Do?

Tina wants to watch TV.
Father says the noise will wake the baby.

Joey wants to wear his new shirt to school.
His brother says to wear an old shirt.

The car will not start.
"We cannot go camping," Father says.
Connie and Jay feel sad.

Gary went to the store for his mother.
On the way home, he lost some money.
Mother wants to know if he bought candy.

A Promise

Lisa likes to climb the fence.
She finds things in the lot.

"Don't climb that fence," says her mother.
Lisa makes a promise to her mother.
"I will not climb the fence," she says.

Rick's turtle is in the lot.
Rick says to Lisa, "Please get my turtle."
"I made a promise to my mother," says Lisa.
"My turtle is my pet," says Rick.
What should Lisa do?

What's Fair?

This class was at recess.
Janie and Richard were throwing rocks.
They broke a school window.
The teacher did not see who did it.

"Who threw the rocks?" asked the teacher.
What should the children do?

What Will Happen?

What would you do?

What is the boy doing?
What will happen?

How does the girl feel?

What do you think will happen?
How would you feel?

UNIT THREE

My Family and My Neighborhood

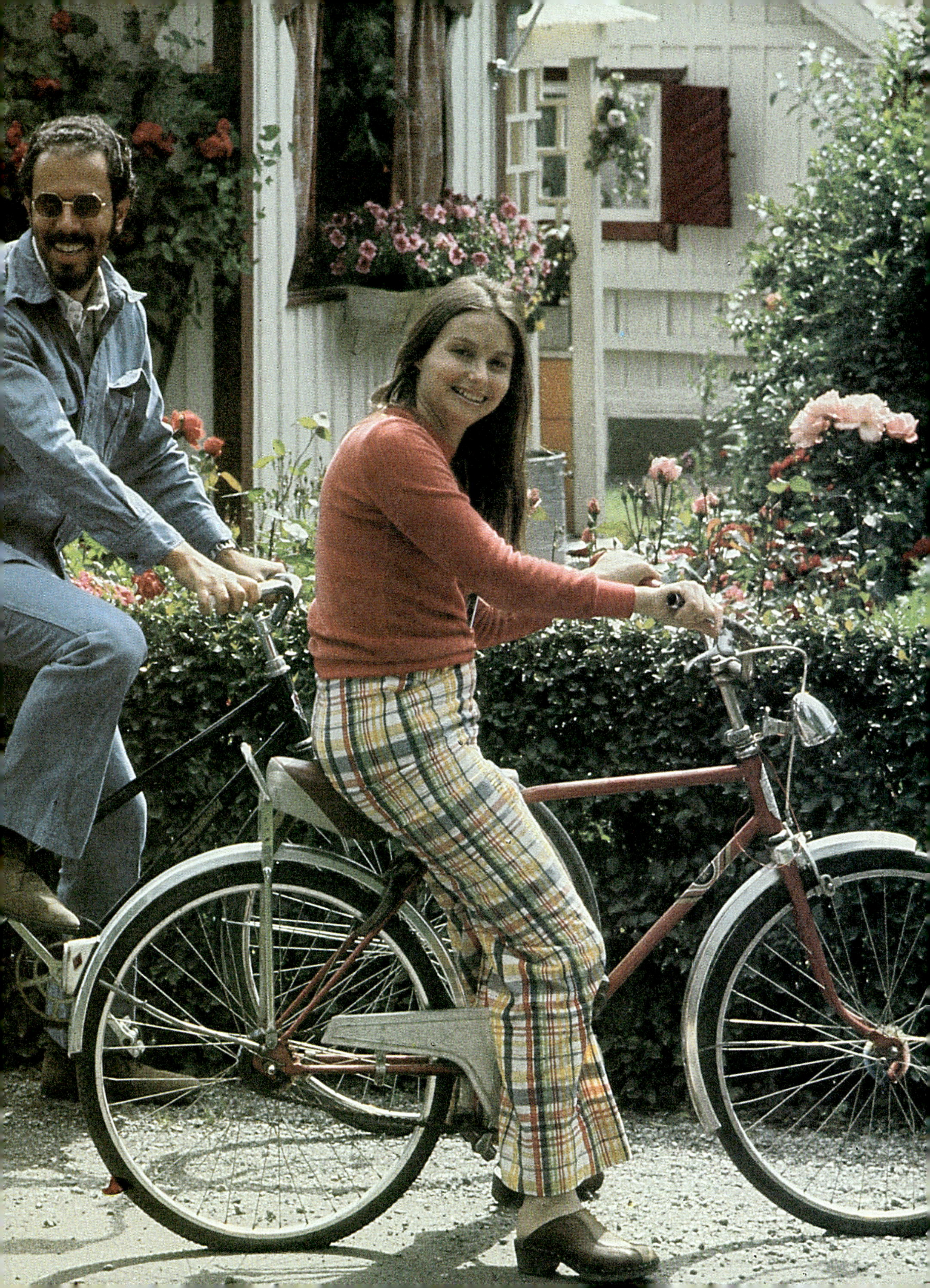

What Is a Family?

These are special groups.

1

2

3

4

5

6

81

What Do Family Members Need?

People need air.

People need water.

People need food.

People need a place to live.

People need clothes.

People need love.

What Do Family Members Do for One Another?

What are these people doing?

84

How are they helping?

85

What Do Families Do Together?

What are these families doing?

What does your family do?

87

Where Do Families Live?

Some families live in a city.

Some families live near a city.

Where Do Families Live?

Some families live on a ranch.

This family lives on a farm.

Where do these families live?

91

What Is All Around Me?

These are rooms in a house.
Which rooms are they?

These are maps of rooms.
Tell what you see on the map.

A School

This is a school.
Can you name the rooms?

94

What do you do in the rooms?

School Neighborhood

This is the school's neighborhood.

What can you find in the neighborhood?
Name as many places as you can.

A Community

Communities are places.

This community has stores and homes.
It has schools.
It has places in which to play.
It has places in which to worship.

Community Workers

Many people work in communities.
Some help keep communities clean.
Some help keep communities safe.

Some people teach children.

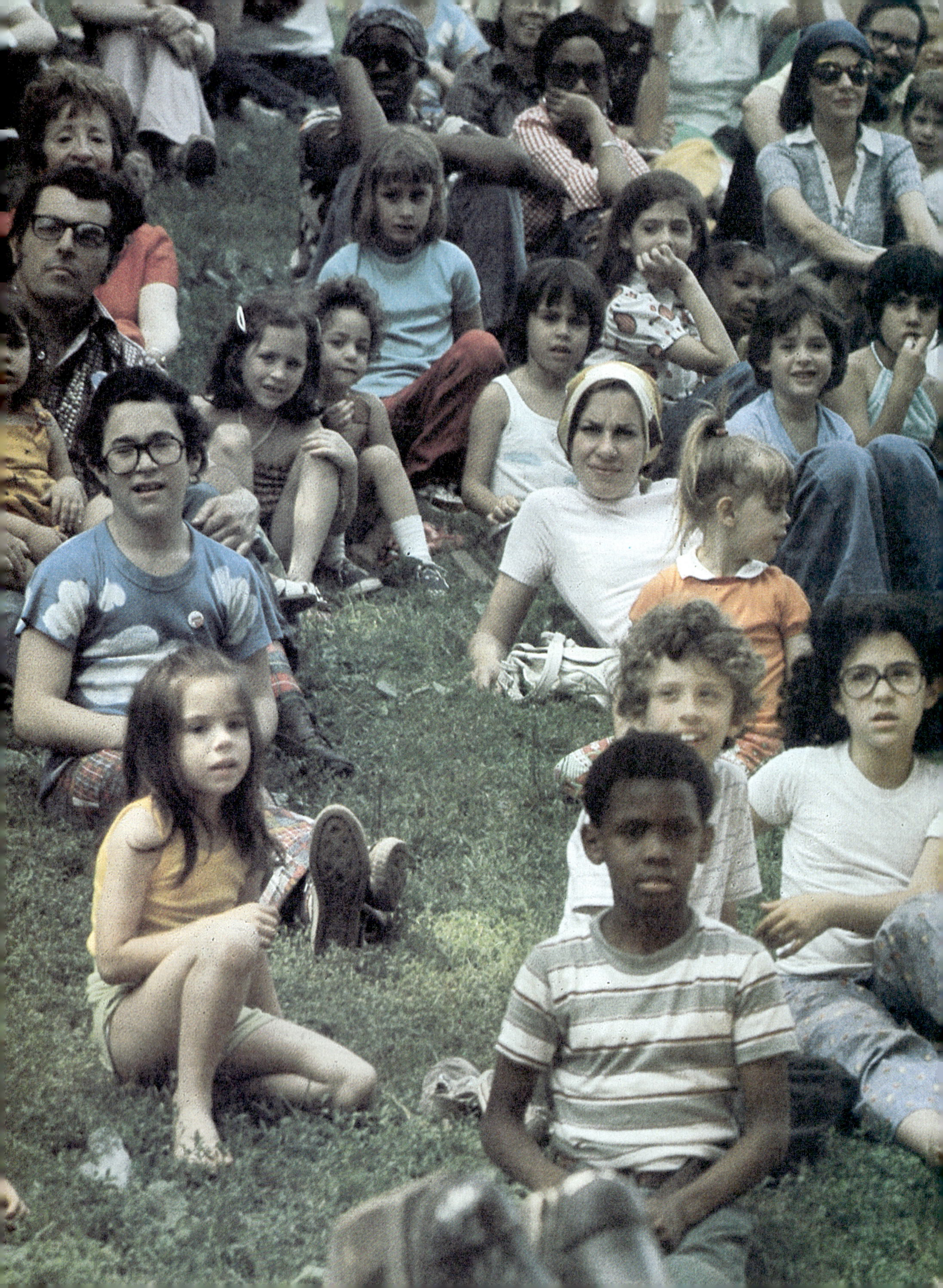

UNIT FOUR

My Country

We Are Americans

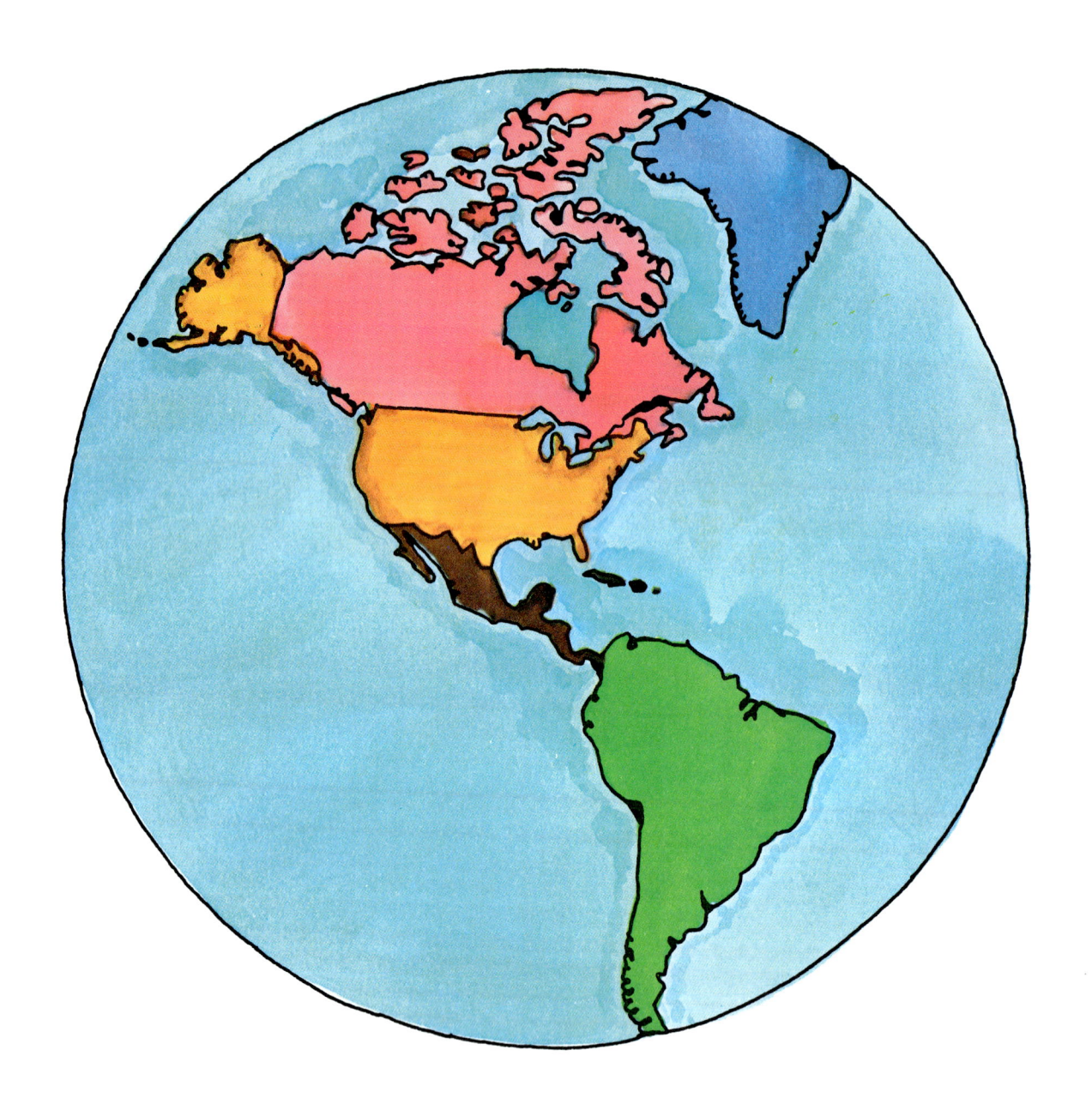

This is a drawing of part of the Earth.
One country is colored orange.
It is called the United States of America.

This is the flag of the United States.
How many stars are there?
How many stripes are there?

Our Capital

This is the Capitol Building.
Laws for all Americans are made here.

This is the White House.
The President lives and works here.
The President is the leader of the country.

Special Days

Our country has many special days. Some are shown here.

Thanksgiving

4th of July

Memorial Day

George Washington's Birthday

Why are these days special?

109

What Do Americans Look Like?

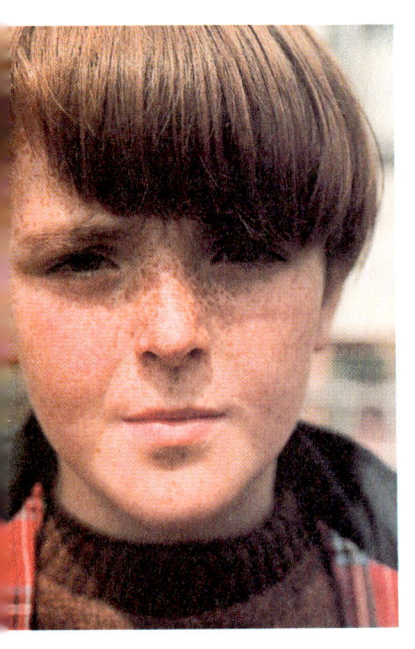

These people are all Americans.
Can you say Americans look alike?
In what ways are Americans alike?

111

Who Are the Native Americans?

Native Americans are Indians.
Native Americans lived in many places.

They lived on the coasts.

They lived in the forests.

They lived in the deserts.

They lived in the grasslands.

How did Native Americans live?

Americans Came from Many Lands

Some came from cities like these.
Some came from farms or villages.
People from many places came to America.

115

Many Different Foods

These are special foods.
Did you ever eat these foods?

Do you ever go out to eat?
What kind of food do you like?

Getting to School

Children go to school in many ways.
Some walk to school.
Some take the school bus.
Some ride in cars.

Can you think of another way?

Long ago there were no cars or buses.
Children walked to school.
Sometimes they walked a long way.
Some children rode horses to school.
Some children rode in buggies.

Schools Then and Now

Today, most schools look like this.
They have big classrooms.
Schools have many rooms.
What rooms do you have in your school?

Long ago, schools looked like this.
They had only one or two classrooms.
All the children were in one room.
What school do you like better? Why?

Cooking Breakfast

This is Lisa Willig.
The girls in the family help cook.

This is Mark Lestor.
He is cooking for his family.

When I Grow Up

What will things be like when I grow up?
What will cars be like?
What will homes be like?
How will people dress?
What will I be like when I grow up?

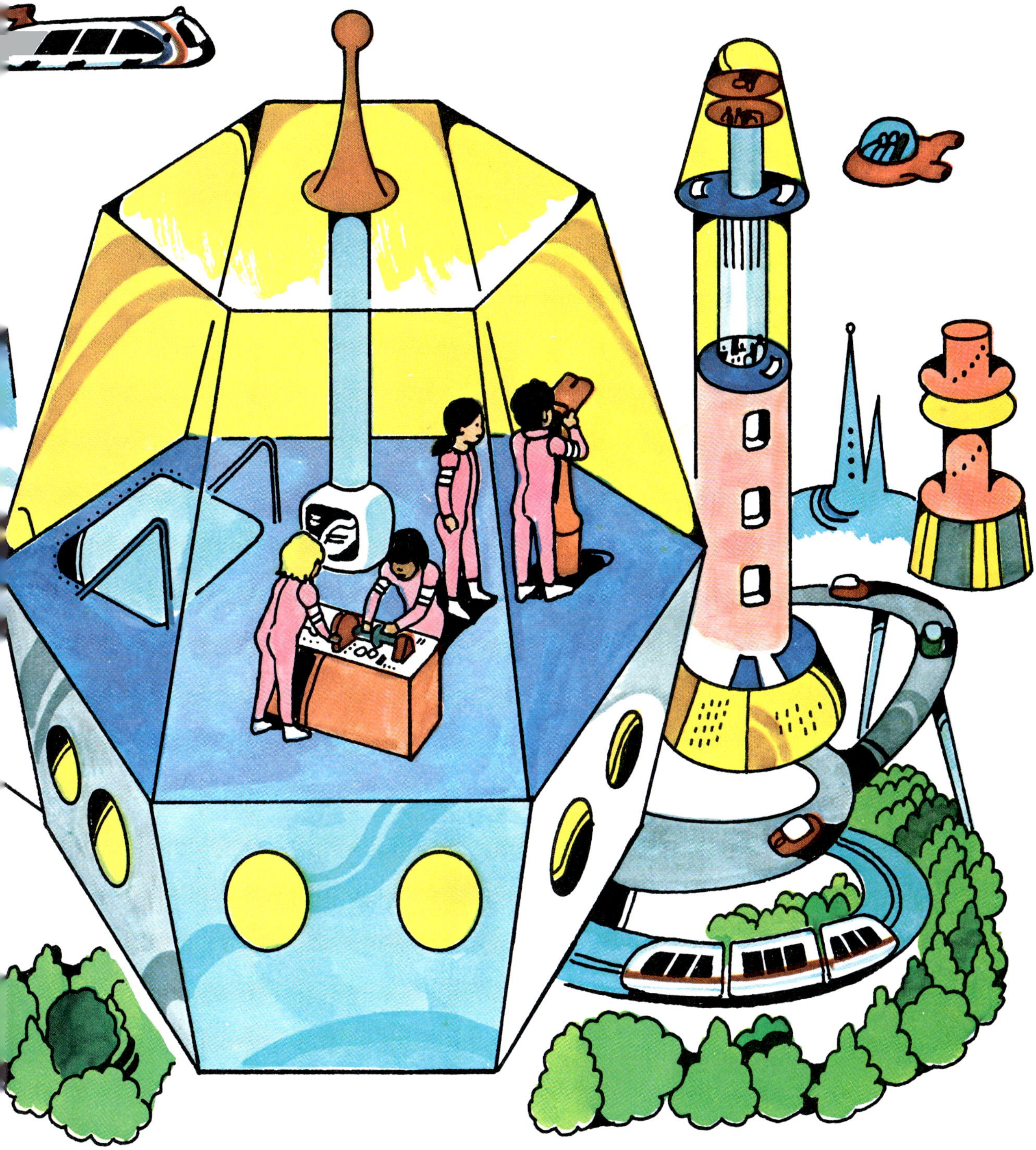

Word Study

alike	alone	bus
camping	change	children
climb	crawl	different
eat	feel	horse
laughing	listening	map

126

message	money	needs
others	people	place
prize	proud	teacher
think	turtle	window
wish	work	worship

CREDITS

Pictures listed clockwise from upper left, unless otherwise noted.

Johnathan Rawle/Stock, Boston: **8–9;** Mike Mazzaschi/Stock, Boston, Cary Wolinsky/Stock, Boston, Michal Heron/Woodfin Camp: **10;** Sylvia Johnson/Woodfin Camp, Richard Nowitz, Erik Anderson/Stock, Boston: **11,** Donald Deitz/Stock, Boston, Frank Siteman/Stock, Boston, Donald Deitz/Stock, Boston: **12;** Ira Kirschenbaum/Stock, Boston, Sam Sweezy/Stock, Boston, Johnathan Rawle/Stock, Boston: **13;** Robert Capece: **14;** Robert Capece: **15;** Robert Capece: **16;** Robert Capece: **17;** Jeffrey J. Foxx/Woodfin Camp: **18;** Owen Franken/Stock, Boston: **19;** Robert Capece: **20;** Robert Capece: **21;** Robert Capece: **22;** Robert Capece: **23;** Daniel Brody/Stock, Boston, Mimi Forsyth/Monkmeyer, Peter Menzel/Stock, Boston: **24;** Michael Collier/Stock, Boston, William Hubbell/Woodfin Camp, Elihu Blotnick/Woodfin Camp: **25;** Owen Franken/Stock, Boston, William Hubbell/Woodfin Camp, William Hubbell/Woodfin Camp: **26;** Peter Vandermark/Stock, Boston, Jeffrey J. Foxx/Woodfin Camp, Mike Mazzaschi/Stock, Boston: **27;** Frank Siteman/Stock, Boston, Mike Mazzaschi/Stock, Boston, Frank Siteman/Stock, Boston: **30;** Frank Siteman/Stock, Boston, Mike Mazzaschi/Stock, Boston, Mike Mazzaschi/Stock, Boston: **31;** Hugh Rogers/Monkmeyer, Lily Solmssen/Photo Researchers: **32;** Marion Faller/Monkmeyer: **33;** Cary Wolinsky/Stock, Boston, Peter Vandermark/Stock, Boston, Donald Deitz/Stock, Boston: **42;** Frank Siteman/Stock, Boston, Mimi Forsyth/Monkmeyer, Jeffrey J. Foxx/Woodfin Camp: **43;** David S. Strickler/Stock, Boston, Anna Kaufman Moon/Stock, Boston, Freda Leinwand/Monkmeyer: **44;** Owen Franken/Stock, Boston, Owen Franken/Stock, Boston, Mimi Forsyth/Monkmeyer: **45;** Frank Siteman/Stock, Boston: **46–47;** Owen Franken/Stock, Boston, Mike Mazzaschi/Stock, Boston, Jeffrey J. Foxx/Woodfin Camp, Mike Mazzaschi/Stock, Boston: **48;** Owen Franken/Stock, Boston, Owen Franken/Stock, Boston, Owen Franken/Stock, Boston, Mike Mazzaschi/Stock, Boston, Richard Nowitz: **49;** J. Gerald Smith/Monkmeyer, Mike Mazzaschi/Stock, Boston, Owen Franken/Stock, Boston: **54;** Owen Franken/Stock, Boston: **55;** Owen Franken/Stock, Boston: **56;** J. Gerard Smith/Monkmeyer, Donald Deitz/Stock, Boston, Olivier Rebbot/Stock, Boston: **57;** Jason Laure/Woodfin Camp, Erik Anderson/Stock, Boston, Mimi Forsyth/Monkmeyer: **60;** Denley Karlson/Stock, Boston, Adam Woodfitt/Woodfin Camp: **61;** Milton Feinberg/Stock, Boston, Owen Franken/Stock, Boston: **62;** Peter Menzel/Stock, Boston, John Marmaras/Stock, Boston, Marvin A. Newman/Woodfin Camp: **63;** Albert Moldvey/Woodfin Camp: **76–77;** Owen Franken/Stock, Boston: **78;** Mimi Forsyth/Monkmeyer: **79;** William Hubell/Woodfin Camp, Michal Heron/Woodfin Camp: **80;** Owen Franken/Stock, Boston, Owen Franken/Stock, Boston, Johnathan Rawle/Stock, Boston, Dan Budnik/Stock, Boston: **81;** Owen Franken/Stock, Boston, Mike Mazzaschi/Stock, Boston, Elihu Blotnick/Woodfin Camp: **82;** Owen Franken/Stock, Boston, Erik Anderson/Stock, Boston, Sam Sweezy/Stock, Boston: **83;** Owen Franken/Stock, Boston, Ginger Chih/Peter Arnold: **84;** Charles Anderson/Monkmeyer, David S. Strickler/Monkmeyer, Hugh Rogers/Monkmeyer: **85;** William Hubbell/Woodfin Camp, Toge Fujihira/Monkmeyer: **86;** Freda Leinwand/Monkmeyer, Mimi Forsyth/Monkmeyer, Elihu Blotnick/Woodfin Camp: **87;** Bill Finch/Stock, Boston, Christopher S. Johnson/Stock, Boston: **88;** Hugh Rogers/Monkmeyer, Hugh Rogers/Monkmeyer, Mike Mazzaschi/Stock, Boston: **89;** Joe Munroe/Photo Researchers, Daniel Brody/Stock, Boston: **90;** Pro Pix/Monkmeyer, Mimi Forsyth/Monkmeyer: **91;** Charles Anderson/Monkmeyer, Owen Franken/Stock, Boston, Nick Passman/Stock, Boston: **100;** Sybil Shackman/Monkmeyer, Daniel Brody/Stock, Boston, A. Devaney/Joan Kramer & Assocs.: **101;** Tim Eagan/Woodfin Camp: **102–103;** Sylvia Johnson/Woodfin Camp, Bill Gillette/Stock, Boston: **106;** Peter Southwick/Stock, Boston: **107;** William Hubbell/Woodfin Camp, Robert DeGast/Photo Researchers: **108;** Peter Southwick/Stock, Boston, J. R. Holland/Stock, Boston: **109;** Mimi Forsyth/Monkmeyer, Frank Siteman/Stock, Boston, Jeffrey J. Foxx/Woodfin Camp, Donald Deitz/Stock Boston, Johnathan Rawle/Stock, Boston: **110;** Erik Anderson/Stock, Boston, Owen Franken/Stock, Boston, Chester Higgins Jr./Photo Researchers, Jeffrey J. Foxx/Woodfin Camp: **111;** Irene Bayer/Monkmeyer: **112;** Culver, Bettmann Archive: **112;** Culver: **113;** Carl Purcell/Photo Researchers, Van Bucher/Photo Researchers: **114;** Thomas Hopler/Woodfin Camp, Erik Anderson/Stock, Boston, Tomas D. W. Friedman/Photo Researchers: **115;** Peter Menzel/Stock, Boston, Ian Yeomans/Woodfin Camp, Mimi Forsyth/Monkmeyer: **116;** Cary Wolinsly/Stock, Boston, Anthony Howarth/Woodfin Camp: **117;** Elihu Blotnick/Woodfin Camp, Joe Molnar/Photo Researchers, Mimi Forsyth/Monkmeyer, Erik Anderson/Monkmeyer: **118;** Bettmann Archive: **119;** Ellis Herwig/Stock, Boston, Hugh Rogers/Monkmeyer: **120;** Culver: **121;** Culver: **122;** Morton Beebe/Image Bank: **123**